Break Every Chain:
A Revolutionary Journey to Emancipation

Eric J. Freeman, PhD

The Freeman Institute

FOR INTEGRATIVE RESEARCH

Copyright © 2025 by Eric J. Freeman
All rights reserved.

Published by
The Freeman Institute for Integrative Research
201 Columbia Mall Blvd.
Columbia, SC 29223

ISBN 979-8-9929512-1-9

No part of this publication may be reproduced, distributed, or transmitted in any form or by any means, including photocopying, recording, or other electronic or mechanical methods, without the prior written permission of the publisher, except in the case of brief quotations embodied in critical reviews and certain other noncommercial uses permitted by copyright law.

First Edition

The Freeman Institute for Integrative Research

This handbook is a product of *The Freeman Institute for Integrative Research*, an interdisciplinary entity dedicated to examining complex theological and societal issues through multiple academic lenses. The Institute focuses particularly on making doctrine accessible, exploring under-researched topics in theological discourse, and incorporating historically marginalized perspectives that contribute to a more comprehensive understanding of Christian faith and practice.

Through its publications and initiatives, the Institute develops accessible, research-informed resources that bridge theoretical theology with practical application. This handbook on doctrine exemplifies the Institute's commitment to integrating biblical truth with contemporary challenges, providing believers with frameworks that foster both theological fidelity and meaningful spiritual growth in an increasingly complex world.

Table of Contents

PREFACE VII

WEEK ONE

RECOGNIZING CHAINS 1

DAY 1 3
UNDERSTANDING SPIRITUAL BONDAGE 3
DAY 2 7
THE DANGER OF ISOLATION 7
DAY 3 11
VOICES THAT BIND 11
DAY 4 15
ACKNOWLEDGING THE NEED FOR DELIVERANCE 15
RECOGNIZING COMMUNITY'S ROLE 19
CHAINS IN PLAIN SIGHT 23
DAY 7 29
RECOGNIZING GOD'S AUTHORITY 29
CLOSING THOUGHT FOR THE WEEK 33

WEEK TWO

UNDERSTANDING LIBERATION 35

DAY 8 37
COMING TO JESUS OPENLY 37
DAY 9 41
JESUS' COMPASSIONATE RESPONSE 41
DAY 10 45
THE POWER OF CHRIST'S AUTHORITY 45
DAY 11 49
BREAKING CULTURAL NORMS 49
DAY 12 53
TESTIMONY AS A TOOL FOR FREEDOM 53
DAY 13 57
REGIONAL AND GENERATIONAL IMPACT 57
DAY 14 61
THE ROLE OF INTERCESSORY PRAYER 61
CLOSING THOUGHT FOR THE WEEK 65

WEEK THREE
PRACTICING FREEDOM 67

DAY 15 69
WALKING IN YOUR AUTHORITY 69
DAY 16 73
SPEAKING TRUTH IN COMMUNITY 73
DAY 17 77
RETURNING HOME CHANGED 77
DAY 18 81
MAINTAINING FREEDOM 81
DAY 19 85
THE POWER OF PERSONAL EVANGELISM 85
DAY 20 89
IMPACTING YOUR COMMUNITY 89
DAY 21 93
LIVING AS A CHAIN BREAKER 93
CLOSING THOUGHT FOR THE WEEK 97

CONCLUSION
"LIVING AS A CHAIN BREAKER" 99

APPENDICES 101

APPENDIX A
SCRIPTURE INDEX FOR FURTHER STUDY 103
APPENDIX B
PRAYER GUIDE FOR BREAKING SPECIFIC TYPES OF CHAINS 105
Prayer for Breaking Addiction 105
Prayer for Breaking Fear and Anxiety 105
Prayer for Breaking Unforgiveness 106
Prayer for Breaking Generational Patterns 107
APPENDIX C
TESTIMONY WORKSHEET FOR DEVELOPING YOUR STORY 109
APPENDIX D
GROUP DISCUSSION GUIDE FOR SMALL GROUP USE 117
Week 1: Recognizing Chains 117
Week 2: Understanding Liberation 119
Week 3: Practicing Freedom 121
APPENDIX E
CHAIN-BREAKING DECLARATION 123

PREFACE

Welcome to *Break Every Chain: A Revolutionary Journey to Emancipation*. This workbook is more than just a daily devotional—it's an invitation to break free from the burdens that bind your spirit, limit your potential, and cloud your relationship with God through the supreme authority of Christ.

Over the next 21 days, you'll journey through three transformative stages: recognizing the chains that bind you, understanding true liberation through Christ's authority, and practicing freedom in your daily life. Each day provides scripture meditation, focused teaching, reflection questions, practical action steps, and guided prayer—all designed to help you confront personal strongholds and empower your journey toward spiritual freedom.

For maximum impact, we encourage you to:

- Set aside consistent daily time for reflection and prayer
- Journal your thoughts in the provided spaces
- Find an accountability partner to share this journey
- Engage honestly with your faith community

Whether you struggle with fear, doubt, past hurts, unhealthy patterns, or spiritual fatigue, this workbook offers biblically grounded insights to help you recognize and dismantle the chains holding you back—not just individually, but in community with others.

As you engage daily with this workbook, prepare to encounter God's unwavering love, grace, and power. The journey may challenge you, but it promises the rich reward of authentic freedom and lasting peace, not just for yourself but potentially for your family, community, and future generations.

Together, let's embark on a powerful journey of faith and liberation. It's time to reclaim your joy, rediscover your purpose, and break every chain through the authority of Christ who sets you free.

Your liberation awaits.

WEEK ONE
RECOGNIZING CHAINS

Welcome to Week 1 of our devotional journey, "Break Every Chain." This week, we will focus on recognizing and understanding the spiritual, emotional, and social chains that may bind us. Recognizing these chains is the crucial first step toward experiencing true freedom in Christ. As we explore the powerful narrative of the demoniac in Mark 5, we'll discover profound truths about spiritual bondage and divine liberation that apply to our own lives today.

Day 1

Understanding Spiritual Bondage

Mark 5:1-5

Spiritual bondage manifests when something other than God exerts control over our lives. In Mark 5, we encounter a man living among the tombs, bound with chains that he repeatedly broke, yet unable to free himself from the spiritual forces controlling him. This vivid picture illustrates how spiritual bondage operates in our lives today.

Bondage rarely announces itself clearly. Instead, it often begins subtly as habits or thought patterns that gradually strengthen their hold until they dominate our choices and behaviors. These chains might appear as persistent anxiety, addiction, unforgiveness, people-pleasing tendencies, materialism, or numerous other manifestations. What makes these chains particularly dangerous is how they isolate us from God's presence and purpose while simultaneously convincing us that we can manage them through our own strength.

The man in the tombs represents an extreme case, but his condition reveals important truths about bondage in our lives. First, spiritual bondage often drives us to destructive behaviors that harm ourselves and others. Second, no amount of physical restraint (chains and shackles) could solve his spiritual problem. Similarly, mere behavior modification cannot address our deeper spiritual needs. Third, his isolation among the tombs separated him from community and healing. Spiritual bondage always attempts to isolate us from those who might help us recognize and break free from our chains.

Recognizing these chains requires honest self-examination and divine illumination. God's Spirit wants to reveal areas where we've surrendered control to something other than Christ, not to condemn us but to guide us toward true freedom.

> ### *Wisdom Reflection*
> "What seems like normal behavior on the surface may actually be evidence of something controlling our lives. True freedom begins when we recognize the difference between our authentic self and the chains that have shaped our actions."

Day 1 Personal Reflections

Date: _____

Reflection: What spiritual or emotional chains can I identify in my life?

_____
_____
_____
_____
_____
_____
_____

Action Taken: Journal the chains I've identified clearly and specifically.

_____
_____
_____
_____
_____
_____

Prayer Focus: Ask God for discernment to clearly see chains in your life.

Day 2

The Danger of Isolation

Proverbs 18:1; Mark 5:2-5

Isolation provides fertile ground for spiritual bondage to flourish. In Mark's account, we find the demoniac living "among the tombs" – a place of death, separation, and ritual uncleanness. This geographical detail reveals a profound spiritual truth: isolation amplifies our vulnerability to spiritual attack and entrenches existing bondage.

The Proverbs text illuminates why isolation is so dangerous: "Whoever isolates himself seeks his own desire; he breaks out against all sound judgment." When we separate ourselves from community, we lose access to the wisdom, accountability, and perspective others provide. Isolation creates an environment where our thoughts remain unchallenged, our struggles remain unshared, and our deceptions remain unexposed. The enemy strategically uses isolation because it removes the protective covering that community provides.

Consider how the demoniac's isolation affected him. Day and night, he was "crying out and cutting himself with stones." Without anyone to intervene, his self-destructive behaviors continued uninterrupted. Similarly, our own chains grow stronger in isolation. Addictions intensify when hidden. Depression deepens when unexpressed. Distorted thinking solidifies when unchallenged.

God's design for humanity has always been community. From Genesis ("It is not good for man to be alone") to the formation of the church, Scripture consistently portrays spiritual health as connected to meaningful relationships. Just as a coal removed from the fire quickly loses its heat, a believer removed from community loses vital spiritual warmth and protection.

Isolation can take many forms beyond physical separation. We can be physically present yet emotionally distant, surrounded by people yet spiritually disconnected. True community requires vulnerability – the willingness to be known authentically, including our struggles and chains. This vulnerability, though frightening, creates the conditions for healing and freedom.

> ### *Wisdom Reflection*
> "When we separate ourselves from supportive community, we open the door to destructive influences. What thrives in darkness often withers when brought into the light of trusted relationships."

Day 2 Personal Reflections

Date: _____

Reflection: How has isolation affected my spiritual health?

_____
_____
_____
_____
_____
_____
_____
_____

Action Taken: Identify individuals or groups I've distanced myself from and why.

_____
_____
_____

Community Element: Who can I reach out to today that I've been avoiding?

_____
_____
_____
_____
_____
_____
_____
_____
_____
_____

Prayer Focus: Ask for courage to reconnect with a godly community.

_____
_____
_____
_____

Day 3
Voices that Bind

Mark 5:9

"My name is Legion, for we are many." This chilling response from the demoniac reveals another important aspect of spiritual bondage – the multiplicity of voices that can influence and control us. While direct demonic possession as portrayed in this narrative may be rare, the principle of multiple negative influences operating in our lives is universally applicable.

Each of us experiences an ongoing chorus of voices competing for authority in our minds and hearts. Some voices originate externally: cultural messages bombard us through media, advertising, and entertainment; family patterns speak through remembered phrases and expectations; peer influences exert pressure through social norms. Other voices emerge internally: our inner critic condemns us; our fears whisper worst-case scenarios; our insecurities highlight our inadequacies. When these voices align with the enemy's agenda rather than God's truth, they function as chains that bind us to patterns contrary to our created purpose.

The name "Legion" referred to a Roman military unit of approximately 6,000 soldiers. This metaphor suggests an overwhelming and coordinated assault on this man's identity and freedom. Similarly, the voices that bind us rarely operate in isolation. Anxiety feeds depression. People-pleasing fuels perfectionism.

Materialism reinforces insecurity. These interconnected voices create a complex web of bondage that can feel impossible to untangle.

Recognizing these voices requires attentive discernment. We must learn to distinguish between God's voice, which always aligns with Scripture and brings clarity even when challenging us, and counterfeit voices that create confusion, condemnation, and chaos. Freedom begins when we identify which voices have been shaping our perceptions, decisions, and behaviors.

> ### *Wisdom Reflection*
> "We often listen to many voices that shape our thoughts and actions. Discerning which voices lead us toward truth and which lead us toward bondage is essential for experiencing freedom."

Day 3 Personal Reflections

Date: _____

Reflection: What negative voices or influences have power over my decisions or emotions?

_____

_____

_____

_____

_____

_____

_____

Action Taken: List the voices or sources that negatively influence me.

_____

_____

_____

_____

Prayer Focus: Ask for discernment to recognize and reject ungodly voices.

Day 4

Acknowledging the Need for Deliverance

Psalm 34:17-19

Deliverance begins with acknowledgment – the honest recognition of our need for divine intervention. This step is often the most difficult because it requires surrendering our illusion of self-sufficiency. The Psalmist understood this when writing, "The Lord is near to the brokenhearted and saves the crushed in spirit." Before we can experience God's saving power, we must acknowledge our brokenness and crushed condition.

In the narrative of the Gerasene demoniac, we see that the man's deliverance began when he encountered Jesus. Mark 5:6 tells us, "When he saw Jesus from afar, he ran and fell down before him." This action represented a pivotal shift. Despite his bondage, something within him recognized Jesus as the source of potential freedom. This recognition propelled him toward the very One who could break his chains.

Many of us struggle with this fundamental acknowledgment for various reasons. Pride convinces us we should be able to overcome our challenges independently. Shame suggests our struggles are uniquely disgraceful and therefore must remain hidden. Fear whispers that admitting our need makes us vulnerable to rejection or judgment. Cultural messages reinforce the ideal of self-reliance and personal strength. All these barriers prevent us from the humble acknowledgment that precedes authentic deliverance.

The paradox of spiritual transformation is that strength begins in acknowledged weakness. As Paul discovered, God's power is "made perfect in weakness" (2 Corinthians 12:9). When we pretend to be strong or hide our struggles, we actually block the flow of divine power available to us. Deliverance requires honest vulnerability before God and often before trusted others who can support our journey toward freedom.

Acknowledging our need isn't a one-time event but an ongoing posture. Even as certain chains break, we maintain humble dependence on God, recognizing that sustainable freedom comes through continued surrender rather than self-reliance.

> ### *Wisdom Reflection*
> "True strength begins when we acknowledge our limitations. Healing starts when we admit our wounds. Freedom comes when we recognize our chains."

Day 4 Personal Reflections

Date: _____

Reflection: What barriers prevent me from admitting my need for God's help?

_____
_____
_____
_____
_____
_____
_____

Action Taken: Write a prayer acknowledging my need for deliverance.

_____
_____
_____
_____

Prayer Focus: Ask for humility to openly admit your need for God's intervention.

Day 5

Recognizing Community's Role

Hebrews 10:24-25

Community isn't merely a helpful addition to our spiritual journey; it's an essential component of God's design for our growth and freedom. The writer of Hebrews instructs believers not to neglect meeting together but rather to encourage one another – a command rooted in God's understanding of how spiritual transformation occurs. This principle applies directly to the process of breaking chains in our lives.

In the narrative of the demoniac, we observe how isolation perpetuated his bondage. Living among the tombs, separated from human contact, his condition remained unchanged until Jesus intervened. After his deliverance, Jesus instructed him to "Go home to your friends and tell them how much the Lord has done for you" (Mark 5:19). This direction wasn't incidental but intentional – Jesus understood that the man's continued freedom would be sustained within community.

Community serves multiple functions in breaking our chains. First, it provides perspective we cannot gain alone. Others can often see our blind spots, identifying patterns and chains we've normalized or rationalized. Second, community offers accountability that strengthens our resolve when facing temptation. Knowing others are walking alongside us adds motivation to resist returning to former bondage. Third, community supplies encouragement when the journey becomes difficult. Breaking long-established chains rarely happens instantly; the process often involves struggles and setbacks that require others' support to navigate successfully.

Additionally, community provides living testimonies that inspire hope. When we witness others experiencing freedom from similar chains, their stories become evidence that our own deliverance is possible. Their victories remind us that God's power is sufficient not only in principle but in practice. Their journeys provide practical wisdom about specific strategies that facilitate breaking particular chains.

The enemy understands these benefits of community, which explains why isolation is often his first strategy. By convincing us that our struggles are unique, shameful, or beyond understanding, he separates us from the very relationships that could facilitate our freedom. Reengaging with authentic community, therefore, represents a direct counterattack against the enemy's tactics.

Wisdom Reflection

"Just as plants need sunlight, water, and nutrients from the soil to flourish, our spiritual growth requires various elements that only community can provide. In isolation, our potential for transformation diminishes significantly."

Day 5 Personal Reflections

Date: _____

Reflection: How has isolation hindered my spiritual growth?

_____

_____

_____

_____

_____

_____

_____

_____

_____

Action Taken: Identify specific communities or relationships to reconnect with spiritually.

_____

_____

_____

Community Element: What concrete steps can I take to engage with my faith community?

_____

_____

_____

_____

_____

Prayer Focus: Ask God to open your heart to receive support and encouragement through others.

_____

_____

_____

_____

_____

_____

_____

Day 6

Chains in Plain Sight

John 8:32

"You will know the truth, and the truth will set you free." These words from Jesus highlight an essential reality about spiritual bondage: liberation begins with recognizing truth. The challenge we face is that many chains binding us have become so normalized by our culture, environment, or personal history that we fail to recognize them as chains at all. Like fish unaware of the water surrounding them, we can be immersed in bondage while perceiving it as normal.

Cultural normalization represents one of the most powerful disguises for spiritual chains. When everyone around us exhibits certain attitudes or behaviors, these patterns can seem acceptable or even desirable despite their destructive nature. Materialism, for example, appears as "financial responsibility" or "enjoying the fruits of hard work" when an entire society practices it. Gossip becomes "sharing concerns" or "processing experiences" when commonly practiced in our social circles. Achievement-based identity transforms into "good stewardship of talents" or "excellence" when celebrated by our community. These reframings obscure the underlying bondage these patterns create.

Familial normalization creates similar blindness. Growing up in environments where certain dysfunctional behaviors were common—whether unhealthy conflict patterns, emotional suppression, performance-based love, or various forms of manipulation—we internalize these dynamics as "just how life works." The chains formed through these experiences often remain invisible precisely because they've shaped our understanding of normal relationships.

Personal normalization occurs when we've lived with certain chains so long that we've incorporated them into our identity. Statements like "I'm just an anxious person" or "I have a quick temper" or "I'm naturally pessimistic" reveal how we can mistake chains for personality traits. When we define ourselves by our bondage, we significantly reduce our capacity to recognize these patterns as foreign impositions rather than authentic identity.

Breaking these normalized chains requires exposure to truth that challenges our perceptions. Scripture provides this corrective lens, revealing God's design for human flourishing that often contrasts sharply with normalized bondage. Authentic community also helps by offering alternative models and gentle confrontation when our "normal" contradicts God's intentions for us. The Holy Spirit works through both Scripture and community to illuminate chains we've mistaken for normal life conditions.

> ### *Wisdom Reflection*
> "What we accept as normal often determines what we will never change. Transformation begins when we question whether what we've always known is actually what God intended."

Day 6 Personal Reflections

Date: _____

Reflection: What normalized chains has God revealed to me this week?

_____

_____

_____

_____

_____

_____

_____

_____

_____

Action Taken: Commit to daily honesty in my prayer life.

_____

_____

_____

Prayer Focus: Ask for clarity to see and reject culturally normalized chains.

_____

_____

_____

_____

_____

_____

Day 7
Recognizing God's Authority
Colossians 2:15

"He disarmed the rulers and authorities and put them to open shame, by triumphing over them in him." This powerful declaration in Colossians reminds us of a fundamental truth essential for breaking chains: Christ has already secured victory over every spiritual force that seeks to bind us. Recognizing and embracing this divine authority constitutes the foundation for experiencing freedom in our daily lives.

In the narrative of the Gerasene demoniac, we witness a dramatic demonstration of Christ's authority. Despite being possessed by a "legion" of demons – suggesting overwhelming spiritual opposition – the man found complete deliverance through a simple command from Jesus. The spiritual forces that had controlled him for years, breaking physical chains and shackles, immediately submitted to Christ's superior authority. This wasn't a hard-fought battle but a decisive assertion of already-established dominion.

This same authority extends to every chain in our lives today. Whether dealing with addiction, fear, unforgiveness, shame, or any other form of bondage, we confront these chains not from a position of weakness hoping to gain victory but from a position of delegated authority based on Christ's accomplished triumph. As believers identified with Christ, we participate in his victory. This profound truth transforms our approach to breaking chains from desperate struggle to confident assertion of what is already established in the spiritual realm.

However, recognizing authority differs from exercising it. Many believers intellectually acknowledge Christ's victory while practically living as though their chains remain unbreakable. The gap between theological understanding and experiential reality often stems from failing to actively appropriate and apply Christ's authority to specific areas of bondage. Faith bridges this gap – not faith as vague spiritual sentiment but as decisive alignment with God's declared reality despite contradicting feelings or circumstances.

The demoniac's story concludes with him "sitting there, clothed and in his right mind" (Mark 5:15). This transformation illustrates the complete restoration available through Christ's authority. The chains that bound him – spiritual, emotional, social, and mental – all yielded to divine authority. Our freedom may unfold more gradually, but the source and extent remain the same: Christ's complete authority over every form of bondage.

Wisdom Reflection

"Freedom doesn't require us to gain new power but to recognize the authority already given to us through Christ. What appears impossible to human strength becomes inevitable when we stand in divine authority."

Day 7 Personal Reflections

Date: _____

Reflection: Do I genuinely believe Christ holds authority over my chains?

_____

_____

_____

_____

_____

_____

_____

_____

_____

Action Taken: Write a personal declaration of Christ's authority over specific struggles.

_____

_____

_____

_____

Testimony Element: Reflect on someone's testimony of experiencing Christ's authority.

_____
_____
_____
_____
_____
_____
_____

Prayer Focus: Ask for faith to believe fully in Christ's authority to break every chain.

_____
_____
_____
_____
_____
_____

Recognizing Chains

Closing Thought for the Week

May you walk forward, recognizing clearly the chains that bind, empowered by the truth of Christ's complete authority over every form of bondage. As this week draws to a close, remember that recognition is the crucial first step in your journey toward freedom. The chains that have bound you—whether visible or hidden, acknowledged or normalized—are now being exposed to the light of God's truth.

This recognition, though sometimes painful, is actually the beginning of hope. For what remains hidden cannot be healed, but what is brought into the light can be transformed by God's power. As you move into the coming week, carry with you the confidence that the same authority that delivered the man among the tombs is available to you through Christ. Your chains have already been defeated at the cross—your journey now is to live in the reality of that victory.

WEEK TWO
UNDERSTANDING LIBERATION

Welcome to Week 2 of our devotional journey, "Break Every Chain." Last week, we focused on recognizing the spiritual, emotional, and social chains that bind us. This week, we will explore the process of liberation through Christ. As we continue studying the powerful narrative of the demoniac in Mark 5, we'll discover how Jesus not only breaks chains but also restores identity, purpose, and community to those He sets free.

Day 8

Coming to Jesus Openly

Mark 5:6

The path to liberation begins with a decisive movement toward Jesus. In Mark 5:6, we see that "when he saw Jesus from a distance, he ran and fell on his knees in front of him." Despite the man's torment and bondage, something within him recognized Jesus as the source of freedom and compelled him to approach.

This movement toward Jesus represents the critical first step in our own liberation. It requires both recognition of our need and willingness to approach Jesus with our brokenness fully exposed. Coming to Jesus is not about presenting our best self or hiding our struggles; it's about bringing our authentic, unchained reality before the One who has the power to transform it.

Notice that the man ran to Jesus "from a distance." Liberation often begins with a distant recognition of Christ's authority, even before we fully understand it. We might feel unworthy, afraid, or uncertain, but that initial movement toward Jesus—however hesitant—opens the door to freedom.

What's remarkable is that despite the demons' control over this man in every other area, they could not prevent him from running to Jesus. Even the strongest chains have a breaking point when confronted with the presence of Christ. Your first step toward freedom may be difficult and may face intense opposition, but

Christ's drawing power can overcome even the most entrenched bondage.

> ### *Wisdom Reflection*
> "The first step toward freedom is often simply approaching Jesus with our authentic selves, complete with our struggles and chains. True courage is found in running toward the Liberator rather than hiding in our bondage."

Day 8 Personal Reflections

Date: _____

Reflection: What holds me back from fully surrendering my chains to Jesus?

_____
_____
_____
_____
_____
_____
_____
_____

Action Taken: Write a personal prayer of surrender.

_____
_____
_____
_____

Prayer Focus: Ask for courage to come to Jesus as you are.

Day 9

Jesus' Compassionate Response

Mark 5:19

When the tormented man approached Jesus, he wasn't met with condemnation, disgust, or rejection. Instead, Jesus responded with compassion and authority, addressing not the man's condition but the forces causing it. This reveals an essential truth about divine liberation: Jesus distinguishes between the person and the chains that bind them.

Many of us fear approaching Jesus with our brokenness because we've internalized a false image of God as condemning rather than compassionate. We equate our struggles with our identity and assume God does the same. But notice how Jesus responded to this man: He never blamed him for his condition or suggested he had brought it upon himself. Instead, Jesus directed His authority against the oppressive forces while treating the man with dignity.

After liberation, Jesus instructs him to "go home to your own people and tell them how much the Lord has done for you, and how he has had mercy on you." Jesus emphasizes mercy—undeserved favor and compassion—as the foundation of the man's freedom. This counters our tendency to believe that freedom must be earned or that only the "worthy" receive deliverance.

Jesus' compassionate response also addresses the man's isolation. By sending him back to "your own people," Jesus begins restoring the community connections that bondage had severed. True liberation isn't just freedom from something but restoration to something—healthy relationships, purpose, and belonging.

> **Wisdom Reflection**
>
> "Jesus distinguishes between the person and the chains that bind them. His compassion addresses our identity while His authority confronts our bondage."

Day 9 Personal Reflections

Date: _____

Reflection: Do I see Jesus as compassionate or condemning? Why?

_____

_____

_____

_____

_____

_____

_____

_____

Action Taken: Meditate on Scriptures about God's compassion (such as Psalm 103).

_____

_____

_____

_____

Prayer Focus: Ask to receive Christ's compassion fully.

Day 10

The Power of Christ's Authority

Luke 10:19

The demoniac's liberation reveals the supreme authority of Christ over every form of bondage. Even a "legion" of demons—representing overwhelming spiritual opposition—immediately submitted to Jesus' command. This display of authority demonstrates a critical truth: no chain is too strong for Christ to break.

In Luke 10:19, Jesus extends this authority to His followers: "I have given you authority to trample on snakes and scorpions and to overcome all the power of the enemy; nothing will harm you." This isn't a symbolic statement but a practical transference of spiritual power. The same authority that broke the demoniac's chains is available to believers today.

Authority differs from power in a significant way. Power relates to ability or strength, while authority relates to right or permission. Jesus possesses both absolute power and unquestionable authority. When we recognize this distinction, we understand that our effectiveness in breaking chains doesn't depend primarily on our personal strength but on the authority delegated to us by Christ.

Exercising this authority requires faith that acknowledges both Christ's absolute power and His delegation of authority to us as His representatives. It means speaking and acting with confidence, not in ourselves, but in the name of Jesus. When we do, chains that have resisted years of human effort can break instantly under divine authority.

> **Wisdom Reflection**
>
> "Authority is not about what we can do, but about what Christ has already done. Our confidence in breaking chains comes not from our strength but from His finished work."

Day 10 Personal Reflections

Date: _____

Reflection: How am I currently exercising spiritual authority in my life?

_____

_____

_____

_____

_____

_____

_____

Action Taken: Practice declaring scriptures of authority over my struggles.

_____

_____

_____

Prayer Focus: Ask for confidence in walking in spiritual authority.

Day 11

Breaking Cultural Norms

Romans 12:2

The demoniac's condition wasn't just an individual problem; it reflected cultural strongholds affecting the entire region. His liberation challenged not only personal bondage but regional patterns that had normalized destructive behaviors. Similarly, our freedom in Christ often requires breaking free from cultural norms that reinforce bondage.

Romans 12:2 instructs us: "Do not conform to the pattern of this world, but be transformed by the renewing of your mind." Cultural patterns often disguise chains as normal or even desirable. What society celebrates—consumerism, individualism, immediate gratification, identity based on achievement—can directly oppose God's design for human flourishing.

Recognizing these cultural chains requires divine perspective. When immersed in a particular culture, we often lack the reference point to identify its destructive patterns. Only by exposing ourselves to God's truth and diverse perspectives beyond our immediate context can we recognize what our culture has normalized.

Breaking cultural norms isn't about rebellion for its own sake but about aligning with Kingdom values even when they contradict societal expectations. It means questioning assumptions about success, relationships, time, resources, and identity that we've unconsciously absorbed. This counter-cultural stance inevitably creates tension but also opens doors for authentic testimony as others notice the freedom that results from this different way of living.

> ### *Wisdom Reflection*
> "What a culture normalizes may directly oppose what God intends. Transformation begins when we question whether what we've always known is actually what God designed."

Day 11 Personal Reflections

Date: _____

Reflection: How has society influenced my views of community, isolation, and independence?

_____
_____
_____
_____
_____
_____
_____
_____

Action Taken: List societal norms I need to challenge to live freely.

_____
_____
_____
_____

Prayer Focus: Ask for courage to stand against cultural chains.

Day 12

Testimony as a Tool for Freedom

Revelation 12:11

After experiencing liberation, Jesus immediately commissioned the former demoniac to "tell how much the Lord has done for you" (Mark 5:19). This wasn't merely an expression of gratitude but a strategic deployment of testimony as a powerful tool for regional freedom. Personal testimony becomes a weapon against corporate bondage.

Revelation 12:11 reveals why testimony carries such power: "They triumphed over him by the blood of the Lamb and by the word of their testimony." Our testimonies of God's liberating work become declarations of Christ's authority that challenge demonic strongholds beyond our personal experience. When we speak about what God has done, we're not just sharing information but releasing transformative power.

Testimonies function as evidence of Christ's authority in specific areas of bondage. When someone who was delivered from addiction shares their story, they provide living proof that freedom is possible for others still in bondage. Their testimony creates a reference point that counters the enemy's lie that "this is just how things are" or "no one ever breaks free from this."

Sharing your testimony isn't optional or secondary to your liberation; it's an essential component that both solidifies your freedom and extends it to others. The enemy knows this, which explains why he tries to silence testimonies through shame, fear, or the suggestion that your experience is too insignificant to share. Every authentic testimony of God's deliverance threatens the enemy's hold over others experiencing similar bondage.

> ### *Wisdom Reflection*
> "Your story of deliverance is not just a personal memory but a powerful declaration of God's character and capability. Every testimony of freedom becomes evidence that others' chains can break too."

Day 12 Personal Reflections

Date: _____

Reflection: What personal testimony do I have that could inspire freedom in others?

_____

_____

_____

_____

_____

_____

_____

_____

Action Taken: Write down my testimony clearly and concisely.

_____

_____

_____

_____

Community Element: Share my testimony with a trusted friend.

Prayer Focus: Ask for boldness to share my story.

Day 13

Regional and Generational Impact

Mark 5:19-20

The scope of Christ's liberating work extends far beyond individual freedom. After the demoniac's deliverance, Mark 5:20 reports that "he went away and began to tell in the Decapolis how much Jesus had done for him. And all the people were amazed." His testimony affected an entire region—ten cities (Decapolis)—demonstrating that personal liberation catalyzes community transformation.

Individual bondage rarely exists in isolation; it typically connects to broader spiritual, social, and generational patterns. Many struggles we face have roots in family systems, cultural beliefs, or historical injustices that span generations. When Jesus breaks our individual chains, He's also addressing these larger patterns and inviting us to participate in more comprehensive liberation.

This regional and generational perspective helps us understand why some chains seem particularly resistant to freedom. Forces that have established strongholds over decades or centuries require persistent, corporate resistance. Your personal deliverance might represent a critical breakthrough in a longer campaign of liberation for your family, community, or geographic region.

Recognizing this broader impact elevates the significance of your liberation story. What God does in your life isn't just about you but potentially about breaking generational patterns that have affected countless others. This perspective helps us persevere through struggles, knowing that our freedom might be securing liberty for generations to come.

> ### *Wisdom Reflection*
> "Personal breakthrough often extends beyond individual freedom to impact families, communities, and future generations. What appears as one person's liberation may actually represent a pivotal shift in a much larger story."

Day 13 Personal Reflections

Date: _____

Reflection: How might my deliverance impact my family or community?

_____
_____
_____
_____
_____
_____
_____
_____

Action Taken: Pray specifically for my family, workplace, or neighborhood.

_____
_____
_____
_____

Prayer Focus: Ask for vision for the broader impact of my freedom.

Day 14

The Role of Intercessory Prayer

James 5:16

James 5:16 teaches, "The prayer of a righteous person is powerful and effective." This principle reveals another essential element of liberation: intercessory prayer. While direct confrontation with spiritual bondage is sometimes necessary, powerful breakthrough often occurs through faithful, persistent prayer for others who are bound.

Intercessory prayer acknowledges that spiritual liberation involves supernatural intervention, not merely human effort or psychological techniques. When we pray for others' freedom, we invite divine power into situations that exceed human capacity to resolve. This posture of dependence aligns us with God's heart and methods.

Effective intercession for the bound combines compassion with authority. We approach God with genuine love for those in bondage while confidently claiming the freedom Christ has already secured. Rather than praying from uncertainty ("If it's Your will..."), we pray from the revealed truth that God desires everyone to be "called out of darkness into his wonderful light" (1 Peter 2:9).

The impact of intercessory prayer often exceeds our awareness. We may never fully know how our prayers contribute to another's liberation, but Scripture assures us that persistent intercession creates spiritual breakthrough. Your faithful prayers for family members, friends, colleagues, or even entire regions experiencing bondage participate directly in God's liberating work.

> ### *Wisdom Reflection*
> "Intercession connects human compassion with divine power. When we pray for others' freedom, we participate in God's liberating work in ways that transcend our understanding and exceed our own abilities."

Day 14 Personal Reflections

Date: _____

Reflection: Who needs my prayers for liberation from bondage?

_____
_____
_____
_____
_____
_____
_____
_____
_____

Action Taken: Dedicate intentional time to intercede for others.

_____
_____
_____
_____
_____

Prayer Focus: Ask for effectiveness in praying for others' deliverance.

Closing Thought for the Week

As this week draws to a close, may you embrace the full process of liberation that Christ offers. Understanding freedom isn't just an intellectual exercise but a transformative experience that changes how you view yourself, others, and God's power. Remember that the same authority that commanded legions of demons to flee is available to you through Christ. Your story of liberation is still being written, and its impact will reach far beyond what you can currently see or imagine. Walk forward in the confidence that "if the Son sets you free, you will be free indeed" (John 8:36).

.

WEEK THREE
PRACTICING FREEDOM

Welcome to Week 3 of our devotional journey, "Break Every Chain." In our first week, we focused on recognizing the spiritual, emotional, and social chains that bind us. Last week, we explored the process of liberation through Christ. This week, we will discover how to walk in and practice the freedom Christ has given us. As we continue studying the powerful narrative of the demoniac in Mark 5, we'll learn practical ways to maintain and expand our freedom while helping others experience liberation as well.

Day 15

Walking in Your Authority

Ephesians 6:10-18

Walking in spiritual authority is not about flexing power or demanding respect—it's about resting in the finished work of Christ and allowing His presence to flow through you. In Ephesians 6, Paul instructs believers to "be strong in the Lord and in his mighty power" and to "put on the full armor of God." This imagery illustrates an important truth about spiritual authority: it doesn't originate with us but comes through our connection to Christ.

When Jesus delivered the demoniac, He didn't announce Himself or make dramatic declarations of power. His very presence was enough to cause the demons to tremble. Similarly, our authority doesn't come from our titles, accomplishments, or spiritual pedigree but from Christ living in us. As we abide in Him, His authority naturally extends through us into every situation we encounter.

Walking in authority requires daily practices that strengthen our awareness of Christ's presence. The spiritual armor Paul describes—truth, righteousness, peace, faith, salvation, and God's Word—creates a spiritual posture that allows Christ's authority to flow unhindered. These aren't religious activities but practical ways of aligning ourselves with Christ's already-established victory.

Many believers struggle with authority because they attempt to generate it themselves through willpower, religious performance, or imitation of others. True authority, however, flows naturally from a deep, abiding relationship with Jesus. When you know who you are in Christ and Whose you are, you don't need to announce yourself or prove your position. Like Jesus, your very presence becomes a catalyst for freedom.

> ### *Wisdom Reflection*
> "True strength begins not in displaying power but in humbly representing the authority that's been entrusted to you. What you possess in Christ is far greater than what you can generate on your own."

Day 15 Personal Reflections

Date: _____

Reflection: How can I walk confidently in my God-given authority today?

_____
_____
_____
_____
_____
_____
_____
_____

Action Taken: Create daily declarations of authority to speak over myself.

_____
_____
_____
_____

Prayer Focus: Ask for confidence in spiritual authority.

Day 16

Speaking Truth in Community

"Therefore each of you must put off falsehood and speak truthfully to your neighbor, for we are all members of one body." This instruction from Paul highlights the transformative power of honest communication within community. For the formerly demon-possessed man, his commission from Jesus was simple yet profound: "Go tell your friends what the Lord has done for you." His testimony wasn't just informational but transformational for the entire Decapolis region.

Speaking truth within community accomplishes several things. First, it solidifies our own freedom. When we verbalize what God has done, we remind ourselves of His power and reinforce our new identity. Second, it creates a testimony that carries spiritual authority. The enemy knows that your testimony gives you power to break the same chains in others' lives, which is why he works so hard to silence it. Third, honest communication builds authentic community where others feel safe to pursue their own liberation.

Many believers keep their journey private, either from shame about their former bondage or from pride about their current freedom. Both extremes undermine God's intention for community. Your story of liberation was never meant to be a private experience but a public testimony that extends freedom to others. When you speak about what God has done, you're not merely sharing information—you're releasing authority that confronts the same chains in others' lives.

The demoniac's obedience to "go tell" resulted in amazement throughout the region. Your honest sharing about both your struggles and victories can similarly transform your sphere of influence. Speaking truth doesn't require eloquence, theological sophistication, or dramatic delivery. It simply requires willingness to be known authentically and to acknowledge God's work in your life.

> ### *Wisdom Reflection*
> "When we speak truth in community, we not only solidify our own freedom but create pathways for others to experience liberation. Honesty breaks the power of isolation that chains thrive in."

Day 16 Personal Reflections

Date: _____

Reflection: How can I speak honestly about my journey to freedom?

_____

_____

_____

_____

_____

_____

_____

Action Taken: Share my journey with a trusted person or group.

_____

_____

_____

_____

_____

Community Element: Plan a time to share my testimony with others.

Prayer Focus: Ask for boldness to speak truth.

Day 17

Returning Home Changed

Mark 5:19-20

After his dramatic deliverance, the former demoniac begged to accompany Jesus. Surprisingly, Jesus refused his request, instructing him instead: "Go home to your own people and tell them how much the Lord has done for you." This command reveals an important principle: genuine freedom must be tested and demonstrated in familiar environments.

It's often easier to live out our freedom among strangers who have no preconceptions about us than among family and friends who remember our former bondage. Yet Jesus intentionally sends this man back to the very community that had witnessed his chains. By returning transformed, his testimony would carry greater weight precisely because these people knew who he had been before.

Returning home changed requires both courage and humility. Courage because old environments often trigger old patterns, and those who knew us before may be skeptical of our transformation. Humility because proving our freedom isn't about demanding recognition but about consistently demonstrating a new way of living. The former demoniac didn't need to announce his freedom—his very presence, now "clothed and in his right mind," was a living testimony.

Many believers seek new environments after experiencing freedom, assuming a fresh start will protect their liberation. While sometimes necessary, this approach can short-circuit God's intent to use your transformation to bring healing to your original community. Jesus doesn't say, "Come with me and leave the region." Instead, He says, "Stay right here in this region" and let your changed life impact those around you.

Your family, workplace, neighborhood, or social circle may be the very "Decapolis" God wants to transform through your testimony. By consistently living your freedom in familiar contexts, you demonstrate that chains truly have been broken, and you extend the possibility of freedom to others still bound by similar forces.

> ### *Wisdom Reflection*
> "True transformation is proven not by escaping difficult environments but by returning to them changed. Your most powerful testimony often emerges in the very places that once witnessed your bondage."

Day 17 Personal Reflections

Date: _____

Reflection: What community or relationships need me to return transformed?

_____

_____

_____

_____

_____

_____

_____

Action Taken: Plan specific steps to re-engage relationships in a healthy way.

_____

_____

_____

_____

Prayer Focus: Ask for wisdom in rebuilding relationships.

Day 18

Maintaining Freedom

Galatians 5:1

"It is for freedom that Christ has set us free. Stand firm, then, and do not let yourselves be burdened again by a yoke of slavery." Paul's exhortation acknowledges an important reality: freedom, once attained, must be actively maintained. Breaking chains is a decisive event, but staying free is an ongoing process.

The formerly demon-possessed man faced a significant challenge after his deliverance. While the dramatic encounter with Jesus broke his immediate bondage, sustaining that freedom would require new habits, thought patterns, and community connections. Similarly, our freedom in Christ isn't automatic or self-sustaining—it requires intentional practices that protect and nurture what God has done.

Maintaining freedom involves several key elements. First, remaining connected to the Source of your freedom through consistent spiritual disciplines. Freedom flows from relationship with Christ, not from religious activities, but certain practices help us remain rooted in that relationship. Second, establishing accountability within community. Isolation was the context for the demoniac's bondage, and it remains the enemy's primary strategy for re-establishing chains. Third, recognizing and rejecting the enemy's attempts to restore old patterns through deception, accusation, or temptation.

Many believers experience temporary freedom only to find themselves gradually drifting back into familiar bondage. This cycle often results from neglecting the practices that sustain freedom. Just as physical healing often requires ongoing care after the initial intervention, spiritual and emotional freedom requires continued attention to protect what God has done.

Standing firm in freedom isn't about perfect performance but about responding quickly when you notice old patterns emerging. Freedom is maintained not through flawless living but through honest acknowledgment of struggles and immediate return to practices that strengthen your connection to Christ and community.

> ### *Wisdom Reflection*
>
> "Freedom is not a destination but a daily journey. What has been liberated must be carefully maintained through vigilance, community, and continued surrender to the One who broke the chains."

Day 18 Personal Reflections

Date: _____

Reflection: What practical steps are needed to avoid re-entering bondage?

_____

_____

_____

_____

_____

_____

_____

_____

Action Taken: Set daily, weekly, and monthly spiritual growth goals.

_____

_____

_____

_____

Community Element: Establish regular accountability with a trusted friend.

_____
_____
_____
_____
_____

Prayer Focus: Ask for vigilance against returning to bondage.

_____
_____
_____
_____
_____
_____
_____

Day 19

The Power of Personal Evangelism

Acts 4:20

"As for us, we cannot help speaking about what we have seen and heard." This declaration from Peter and John captures the natural evangelistic impulse that flows from a genuine encounter with Christ. For the delivered demoniac, telling others about his experience wasn't an obligation but an overflow of gratitude and amazement.

Personal evangelism flows most effectively not from memorized presentations or theological arguments but from authentic testimony about what God has done in your life. When the formerly possessed man began telling others throughout the Decapolis about Jesus, he wasn't delivering rehearsed messages but simply sharing his undeniable experience. This form of evangelism carries unique power because it's personal and irrefutable.

Your testimony functions as a bridge between others' needs and God's solution. When you share what God has done for you, you're not merely conveying information but offering evidence that freedom is possible. For those struggling with the same chains that once bound you, your story creates hope that transformation is real and available. This "show, don't just tell" approach to evangelism aligns with how Jesus often worked, using tangible demonstrations of freedom to reveal spiritual truths.

Many believers hesitate to share their faith because they feel inadequately trained or theologically unprepared. Yet the most effective evangelism often comes from those who simply report what God has done, regardless of their spiritual maturity or biblical knowledge. The simplicity of "come and see what happened to me" creates an invitation that's difficult to dismiss.

The demoniac's evangelistic activity—telling others about Jesus throughout the ten cities of Decapolis—created a revival of sorts. Your consistent sharing about God's work in your life can similarly prepare the ground for broader spiritual awakening in your sphere of influence.

> ### *Wisdom Reflection*
> "Your story of deliverance may be the key that unlocks someone else's prison. When we share authentically what God has done, we offer not just information but invitation to experience the same freedom."

Day 19 Personal Reflections

Date: _____

Reflection: How comfortable am I sharing my liberation story with others?

_____

_____

_____

_____

_____

_____

_____

_____

Action Taken: Practice sharing my testimony succinctly.

_____

_____

_____

_____

Prayer Focus: Ask for courage to evangelize through my testimony.

Day 20

Impacting Your Community

Matthew 5:14-16

"You are the light of the world. A town built on a hill cannot be hidden... let your light shine before others, that they may see your good deeds and glorify your Father in heaven." Jesus' words establish a profound truth: personal freedom is meant to catalyze community transformation.

The delivered demoniac didn't just experience private healing but became an agent of regional change. As he moved throughout the Decapolis sharing his testimony, he was dismantling the very spiritual strongholds that had once controlled him. Your freedom similarly carries potential beyond your personal experience—it can become a catalyst for breaking chains at a community level.

Community impact flows from consistent presence and genuine service. When believers allow their freedom to be visible through both their words and actions, they create multiple points of contact where others can encounter Christ. This doesn't require grand platforms or extensive resources but simple faithfulness in sharing your story while demonstrating Christ's love in practical ways.

Many spiritual strongholds operate at a community or regional level, creating patterns of bondage that affect entire populations. These systemic chains—whether addiction, violence, poverty, or spiritual apathy—often seem too entrenched for individual impact.

Yet history repeatedly shows that community transformation often begins with a single liberated person whose testimony creates a ripple effect of freedom.

Your neighborhood, workplace, school, or social network represents your "Decapolis" —the region where your freedom story can catalyze broader transformation. By intentionally engaging these contexts with both testimony and service, you extend Christ's chain-breaking power beyond your personal experience and invite others into the same freedom you've discovered.

> ### *Wisdom Reflection*
> "Individual transformation ultimately creates ripples throughout entire communities. As light dispels darkness without effort, a life freed from chains naturally illuminates possibilities for others still bound."

Day 20 Personal Reflections

Date: _____

Reflection: How might God use my testimony to change my community?

_____
_____
_____
_____
_____
_____
_____
_____

Action Taken: Identify opportunities to serve or speak in my community.

_____
_____
_____
_____

Community Element: Plan a community service project to demonstrate Christ's love.

Prayer Focus: Ask for vision for community impact.

Day 21

Living as a Chain Breaker

Isaiah 61:1-3

"The Spirit of the Sovereign LORD is on me, because the LORD has anointed me to proclaim good news to the poor. He has sent me to bind up the brokenhearted, to proclaim freedom for the captives and release from darkness for the prisoners..." These words, which Jesus applied to His own ministry, now extend to every believer who has experienced His freedom.

The delivered demoniac transitioned from being chain-bound to becoming a chain-breaker throughout the Decapolis region. His story vividly illustrates how God transforms former captives into liberators who extend freedom to others. This progression from liberated to liberator represents God's intention for everyone who experiences Christ's freedom.

Living as a chain-breaker involves several key elements. First, maintaining your own freedom through continued connection with Christ. You cannot lead others where you haven't gone yourself. Second, developing spiritual sensitivity to recognize chains in others' lives without judgment or condemnation. Jesus distinguished between the demons and the demoniac, addressing the spiritual forces without condemning the man. Third, using your testimony as an instrument of liberation that creates hope and demonstrates possibilities for those still bound.

Many believers settle for enjoying their personal freedom without embracing their role in liberating others. Yet the fullness of Christian maturity includes participating in Christ's ongoing mission of proclaiming "freedom for the captives." Just as Jesus doesn't simply enjoy fellowship with the Father but extends that relationship to others, we're called to share our freedom rather than merely experiencing it.

Your journey from bondage to freedom qualifies you uniquely to help others along the same path. Your familiarity with specific chains gives you authority when addressing those same bondages in others' lives. As you embrace this identity as a chain-breaker, you fulfill one of the primary purposes for which God set you free: that you might become an instrument of liberation for others.

Wisdom Reflection

"The greatest evidence of complete freedom is becoming an agent of liberation for others. What God heals in us individually, He intends to use for collective restoration of those around us."

Day 21 Personal Reflections

Date: _____

Reflection: In what areas is God calling me to become a liberator for others?

_____

_____

_____

_____

_____

_____

_____

_____

Action Taken: Write a commitment statement for ongoing personal growth and community involvement.

_____

_____

_____

_____

Community Element: Share what I've learned with someone else.

Prayer Focus: Ask to be commissioned as Christ's ambassador of freedom.

Closing Thought for the Week

As this three-week journey draws to a close, may you walk forward not only free from chains but also actively participating in Christ's ministry of liberation. Your story of deliverance is both a personal testimony and a powerful instrument for extending freedom to others. Remember that the same Christ who broke your chains now lives in you, making you a carrier of His chain-breaking presence wherever you go. As you practice your freedom daily through walking in authority, speaking truth, maintaining vigilance, sharing your testimony, and serving your community, you become a living demonstration of Christ's victory over every form of bondage. Your life is now a declaration that chains can be broken, freedom can be maintained, and what God has done for you, He can do for others.

Conclusion

"Living as a Chain Breaker"

As we conclude our 21-day journey of "Break Every Chain," let us walk forward not only free from chains but also actively participating in Christ's ministry of liberation. Throughout these weeks, we've traveled from recognizing our chains, to understanding God's process of liberation, to practicing freedom daily. The story of the demoniac in Mark 5 has revealed profound truths about spiritual bondage and divine liberation that apply directly to our lives today.

Remember that your story of deliverance is both a personal testimony and a powerful instrument for extending freedom to others. The same Christ who broke the demoniac's chains and commissioned him to "go tell" now lives in you, making you a carrier of His chain-breaking presence wherever you go. When you share what God has done in your life, you're not merely conveying information but releasing authority that directly confronts the same chains in others' lives.

As you practice your freedom daily through walking in spiritual authority, speaking truth in community, maintaining vigilance, sharing your testimony, and serving others, you become a living demonstration of Christ's victory over every form of bondage. The testimony of your transformed life becomes evidence that chains can be broken—not through your own strength, but through the finished work of Jesus Christ.

Your journey from captivity to freedom has uniquely positioned you to help others along the same path. Your familiarity with specific chains gives you authority when addressing those same bondages in others' lives. As Jesus told the delivered man, "Go home to your own people and tell them how much the Lord has done for you, and how he has had mercy on you," so He commissions you to return to your "Decapolis" —your sphere of influence—and extend the freedom you've received.

May the Chain Breaker continue to work through you, bringing liberation not just to individuals but to families, communities, and future generations. Walk confidently in the truth that "if the Son sets you free, you will be free indeed" (John 8:36), and become an agent of that liberating power for others.

APPENDICES

APPENDIX A
Scripture Index for Further Study

Spiritual Bondage and Freedom
- John 8:31-36 - Truth that sets free
- Romans 6:6-14 - Freedom from sin's power
- Galatians 5:1-15 - Standing firm in freedom
- 2 Corinthians 3:17 - Where the Spirit is, there is freedom
- Isaiah 61:1-4 - Proclaimed freedom for captives
- Psalm 107:10-16 - Breaking chains of prisoners
- Acts 12:5-11 - Peter's chains falling off
- Romans 8:1-17 - Life in the Spirit
- Ephesians 4:17-32 - Putting off old self, putting on new
- 1 Peter 2:9-10 - Called out of darkness into light

Authority in Christ
- Luke 10:17-20 - Authority over all power of enemy
- Ephesians 1:15-23 - Christ's authority and power
- Colossians 2:9-15 - Fullness in Christ
- Matthew 28:18-20 - All authority given to Christ
- James 4:7 - Resist the devil and he will flee
- 1 John 4:4 - Greater is He that is in you
- Philippians 2:9-11 - Name above every name
- 2 Corinthians 10:3-5 - Weapons of warfare
- Romans 16:20 - God will crush Satan under your feet

- Revelation 12:10-11 - Overcoming by blood of Lamb and word of testimony

Community and Restoration
- Ecclesiastes 4:9-12 - Two are better than one
- Hebrews 10:24-25 - Not giving up meeting together
- James 5:13-16 - Confessing to one another, prayer for healing
- Galatians 6:1-2 - Carrying each other's burdens
- Proverbs 27:17 - Iron sharpens iron
- Acts 2:42-47 - Early church community
- 1 Corinthians 12:12-27 - One body, many parts
- Romans 12:3-16 - Using gifts in community
- 1 Peter 4:8-11 - Loving each other deeply
- Matthew 18:15-20 - Restoration in community

APPENDIX B

Prayer Guide for Breaking Specific Types of Chains

Prayer for Breaking Addiction

Father God, I acknowledge my powerlessness over this addiction and my need for Your deliverance. I confess that I have allowed this substance/behavior to control me rather than surrendering control to You. In the name of Jesus Christ, I break the power of this addiction in my life. I claim the authority You have given me through Christ to stand against this bondage. Fill me with Your Holy Spirit and strengthen me when temptation comes. Lead me to the support and accountability I need. Thank You that whom the Son sets free is free indeed.

Scripture Declarations:

- "It is for freedom that Christ has set us free." (Galatians 5:1)
- "I can do all things through Christ who strengthens me." (Philippians 4:13)
- "No temptation has overtaken you except what is common to mankind. And God is faithful; he will not let you be tempted beyond what you can bear." (1 Corinthians 10:13)

Prayer for Breaking Fear and Anxiety

Heavenly Father, I come before You acknowledging the fear and anxiety that has controlled my thoughts and actions. I recognize these as chains that have kept me from walking in the freedom You desire for me. In the name of Jesus, I break these chains of fear. I reject the spirit of fear and claim the spirit of power, love, and sound mind that You have given me. Fill my mind with Your truth and peace that surpasses understanding. I choose to fix my thoughts on what is true, honorable, right, pure, lovely, and admirable. I trust You with my future and receive Your perfect love that casts out all fear.

Scripture Declarations:

- "For God has not given us a spirit of fear, but of power and of love and of a sound mind." (2 Timothy 1:7)
- "Cast all your anxiety on him because he cares for you." (1 Peter 5:7)
- "Do not be anxious about anything, but in every situation, by prayer and petition, with thanksgiving, present your requests to God. And the peace of God, which transcends all understanding, will guard your hearts and your minds in Christ Jesus." (Philippians 4:6-7)

Prayer for Breaking Unforgiveness

Lord Jesus, I come before You with the heavy burden of unforgiveness toward [name/situation]. I acknowledge that holding onto this hurt has become a chain in my life, affecting my relationship with You and others. Today, I choose to forgive as You have forgiven me. I release [name] from the debt I believe they owe me. I surrender my right to hold this offense against them. Break the chains of bitterness, resentment, and anger that have bound me. Fill me with Your love and healing. Give me eyes to see them as You see them. Though this may be a process, I commit to walking in forgiveness by Your grace and strength.

Scripture Declarations:

- "Bear with each other and forgive one another if any of you has a grievance against someone. Forgive as the Lord forgave you." (Colossians 3:13)
- "Get rid of all bitterness, rage and anger, brawling and slander, along with every form of malice. Be kind and compassionate to one another, forgiving each other, just as in Christ God forgave you." (Ephesians 4:31-32)
- "For if you forgive other people when they sin against you, your heavenly Father will also forgive you." (Matthew 6:14)

Prayer for Breaking Generational Patterns

Heavenly Father, I thank You that in Christ I am a new creation. Today I stand against the generational patterns of [specific issue] that have affected my family line. I claim the power of the cross of Jesus Christ over these patterns and break their influence in my life and in the lives of my children and future generations. I renounce any participation in these patterns and choose a different path aligned with Your Word and will. Fill me with Your Spirit and give me wisdom to establish new, godly patterns in my life and family. I claim Your promise that the curse is broken through Christ's redemptive work.

Scripture Declarations:

- "Therefore, if anyone is in Christ, the new creation has come: The old has gone, the new is here!" (2 Corinthians 5:17)
- "Christ redeemed us from the curse of the law by becoming a curse for us." (Galatians 3:13)
- "You show love to thousands but bring the punishment for the parents' sins into the laps of their children after them." (Jeremiah 32:18)

APPENDIX C

Testimony Worksheet for Developing Your Story

Your Story of Deliverance

Part 1: Before Christ's Intervention Describe your condition before Christ broke your chains. What were you struggling with? How did it affect your life? (Be honest but avoid details that might trigger others.)

_____

_____

_____

_____

_____

_____

_____

_____

_____

_____

_____

_____

Part 2: How You Encountered Jesus How did you come to recognize your need for Christ's deliverance? Was there a specific moment or a gradual realization? Who or what did God use to help you see your need?

_____

_____

_____

_____

_____

_____

_____

_____

_____

_____

_____

_____

_____

Part 3: The Breaking of Chains Describe how Jesus broke your chains. What happened? What did He specifically deliver you from? How did you experience His power and authority?

_____
_____
_____
_____
_____
_____
_____
_____
_____
_____
_____
_____
_____
_____
_____

Part 4: Life After Deliverance How has your life changed since experiencing freedom in Christ? What new patterns or habits have replaced the old chains? How has your relationship with God and others been affected?

Appendix C

Part 5: Ongoing Journey What challenges have you faced in maintaining your freedom? How has God helped you stand firm? What practices or supports have been most helpful?

_____

_____

_____

_____

_____

_____

_____

_____

_____

_____

_____

_____

_____

_____

_____

Refining Your Testimony for Sharing

One-Minute Version Practice sharing the key points of your testimony in about one minute:

_____
_____
_____
_____
_____
_____
_____
_____
_____
_____

Key Scripture That Relates to Your Story Write down 2-3 verses that connect with your testimony:

1. _____
2. _____
3. _____

Appendix C

People or Situations Where Your Testimony Might Help

List specific types of people or situations where your story might offer hope:

_____

_____

_____

_____

_____

_____

_____

APPENDIX D

Group Discussion Guide for Small Group Use

Week 1: Recognizing Chains

Opening Prayer: (5 minutes)

Begin with prayer asking the Holy Spirit to guide your discussion and create a safe space for sharing.

Scripture Reading: Mark 5:1-5 (5 minutes)

Read the passage aloud. Consider reading from two different translations.

Discussion Questions: (30-40 minutes)

1. What chains do you see in the man described in these verses? How were they manifested?
2. What chains have you recognized in your own life? How did you come to recognize them?
3. How has isolation played a role in strengthening chains in your life or the lives of others you know?
4. What "voices" (influences, messages) have shaped your decisions and self-perception? Which of these align with God's truth and which don't?
5. What makes it difficult to acknowledge our need for deliverance?
6. How has community helped you recognize chains in your life that you couldn't see on your own?

Application: (10 minutes)

1. This week, what is one specific chain you feel God is calling you to address?
2. What practical step can you take to move toward freedom in this area?
3. How can this group support you in this process?

Closing Prayer: (5-10 minutes) Pray for one another specifically regarding the chains identified during discussion.

Appendix D

Week 2: Understanding Liberation

Opening Prayer: (5 minutes)

Scripture Reading: Mark 5:6-15 (5 minutes)

Discussion Questions: (30-40 minutes)

1. What stands out to you about how the demoniac approached Jesus? What might this teach us about coming to Jesus with our own chains?
2. How does Jesus respond to the man's brokenness? How does this challenge or confirm your view of how God responds to our struggles?
3. What does this passage reveal about Jesus' authority? How does this encourage you regarding your own situation?
4. What cultural norms or expectations have reinforced chains in your life?
5. How has hearing others' testimonies of God's deliverance impacted your faith? Can you share an example?
6. In what ways might your personal deliverance affect your family, community, or future generations?

Application: (10 minutes)

1. How can you actively position yourself to receive Christ's liberating power this week?
2. Is there someone who needs to hear your testimony of what God has done in your life?
3. What specific area can we pray for regional or generational impact in your situation?

Closing Prayer: (5-10 minutes) Pray for one another to experience the liberating power of Christ in their lives.

Appendix D

Week 3: Practicing Freedom

Opening Prayer: (5 minutes)

Scripture Reading: Mark 5:18-20 (5 minutes)

Discussion Questions: (30-40 minutes)

1. Why do you think Jesus told the man to go home rather than allowing him to come with Him? What does this teach us about practicing our freedom?
2. What practical disciplines or habits help you walk confidently in your God-given authority?
3. How comfortable are you sharing your story of deliverance with others? What holds you back?
4. What community or relationships might God be calling you to re-engage with as a changed person?
5. What challenges have you faced in maintaining your freedom, and how have you addressed them?
6. How might God want to use your personal testimony to impact your broader community?

Application: (10 minutes)

1. This week, with whom will you share your testimony of what God has done for you?
2. What daily practice will you establish to maintain your freedom?
3. How can you begin to become a "chain breaker" for others?

Closing Prayer: (5-10 minutes) Pray for one another to walk in freedom and to become agents of liberation for others.

APPENDIX E

Chain-Breaking Declaration

I, _____, declare that through the finished work of Jesus Christ:

I am free from the chains of sin and death. I am clothed in my right mind. I am seated with Christ in heavenly places. I am filled with the Holy Spirit. I am equipped with spiritual authority over all the power of the enemy. I am commissioned to share my testimony of deliverance. I am called to be an agent of liberation in my family and community. I am determined to maintain my freedom through God's Word and Christian community. I am living as a chain breaker through the power of Jesus Christ.

I declare that what God has set free is free indeed. I will walk daily in this freedom, guarding it with vigilance, strengthening it with truth, and extending it to others through my testimony and service.

Signed: _____

Date: _____

Witness: _____

About the Author

Eric J. Freeman, PhD (Homiletics and Social Ethics, Anderson University), MA (Theological Ethics, Lutheran Theological Southern Seminary), BS (Finance, University of Florida), is a scholar-practitioner with over 30 years of ministry experience. As a bishop within the Christian Covenant Fellowship of Ministries and founder and Senior Pastor of The Meeting Place Church of Greater Columbia, he has led the transformation of a 23-acre campus into a vibrant hub for community engagement and social impact.

Dr. Freeman's academic and ministerial work converge in his pioneering development of the Evangelical Emancipatory Homiletics™ framework—a theological and homiletical approach emerging from his decades of pastoral preaching, scholarly reflection, and historical research. His preaching and scholarship critically engage under-examined societal issues through a biblical lens, bridging rigorous theology with practical action and advocacy. Named 2023 Humanitarian of the Year by the South Carolina State Conference of the NAACP, Dr. Freeman embodies a deep commitment to empowering believers to live out gospel truths with integrity, compassion, and social responsibility.

He and his wife, Coleen, are the proud parents of two adult children.

The Freeman Institute

FOR INTEGRATIVE RESEARCH

www.ingramcontent.com/pod-product-compliance
Lightning Source LLC
Chambersburg PA
CBHW032055090426
42744CB00005B/227